PARTICLE PIÑATA POEMS

Messages to the Earth:
Guides, Initiations, Word Play
In Partnership with the Spirit World

Margaret A. Harrell

Curated by Alice Osborn: https://aliceosborn.com/

Some of this poetry previously appeared in some version in the *Love in Transition/
Space Encounters* series.

ISBN: 979-8-9860526-0-1

Book cover and interior designed by Deborah Perdue,
https://illuminationgraphics.com/

Cover image, *Faces in Sun Blast* by the author. A detail from *Scenes in Hiding*.

This silver halide (film, not digital) photograph of a cloud scene was exhibited in
October 2020 at the White Space Chelsea Gallery in New York City in an Italy-
curated show. Illustrations other than *Scenes in Hiding* are details from it.

A Published in Heaven Series Book
Published in Heaven Books include titles by His Holiness The Dalai Lama,
President Jimmy Carter, Thomas Merton, Seamus Heaney, Hunter S.
Thompson, Jack Kerouac, Andy Warhol, Allen Ginsberg, Yoko Ono, William S.
Burroughs, Edvard Munch, Diane di Prima, Jim Carroll, Amiri Baraka, Gregory
Corso, John Updike, Rita Dove, Wendell Berry, David Amram, Douglas Brinkley,
BONO, Ron Whitehead, Lawrence Ferlinghetti, and many more.

Published in conjunction with Saeculum University Press
of Sibiu, Romania, and Raleigh, North Carolina

Contents

Consider what you have in the smallest chosen library. A company of the wisest and wittiest men that could be picked out of all civil countries in a thousand years have set in best order the results of their learning and wisdom.

The men themselves were hid and inaccessible, solitary, impatient of interruption, fenced by etiquette; but the thought which they did not uncover to their bosom friend is here written out in transparent words to us, the strangers of another age.

—Ralph Waldo Emerson

I become a transparent eye-ball; I am nothing; I see all; the currents of the Universal Being circulate through me; I am part and parcel of God.

—Emerson

Opening Salvo

What? That spot of dust over there
That leaf on a tree
That sentence that spouted out of someone's mouth
That color red put on by a person when I wore red
Were "my" ideas appearing out there somewhere else?
So how to do it?
How to establish that
Yes, I am
One with God and God is
One with You

Author's Note

This collection of writings, going back to 1985, was in the energies working tirelessly to see long sightedly timelessly and specifically into the twenty-first century. Predictive, seeing ahead.

Consciousness whispering to me even then that change was afoot (as it always is, but bigtime). Carrying this baton. How to, in belatedly publishing it, make it relevant, important, even now—can I?

How to interest a modern reader, which includes myself? But then, I'm interested—can't let go as I'm pulled sky-high, cosmos-high, stretched out (that's for sure) beyond everything I know sometimes. Who am I there (because I definitely find myself there too)? Even I had reluctance to give these writings attention. Which they deserve, of course, but what slant to use? I've always been a poet without exactly knowing it, except at seven years old, writing my first poetry book. A child's scribblings, her message to me not to forget the poet.

I dare say it scarcely counted to some spiritual part of me (or not) who accosted me on the road, just steps from my house—with a woods to my right, as in the first stanza of Dante's *Divine Comedy*. As from inside my own body this unknown spirit took over, proclaiming to himself (and me) his identity as a "great" writer, nameless (fancy that). And what had he to do with me, a tiny child, except that he was using my mind to think in, the very boundaries of my brain being, in his "mind" his own. He didn't know how he possibly got inside my body, and certainly I, frozen in my tracks, hadn't a clue.

Much later the track picked up, but in dreams (pouring in in 1980), when I lived (excessively bored) in Morocco—pointing me to "image trails." Since a part of me thought in images, to reach me with images was child's play. Indeed. Some images, I traced back to Le Dôme Café in Montparnasse, Paris, 1965. I had gone to that café to follow the steps of Hemingway and other novelists (I was trying to—at last—put pen, or rather cumbersome Underwood typewriter, to paper in writing my Big Book). I went to soak up the atmosphere, become drenched in it, of these great writers and artists' torments, their poverty, their brilliance—the energy still faintly vibrating, it felt like, in their very café seats. That should get me started.

The intent set much in motion—my unconscious being, always, one step or ten steps ahead. At the café, that intent seized on a signal, numinously, subliminally again urging me on, but this time it was outside me—in the form of a tall, tattered, gangly beggar. This "tramp" reminding me of Charlie Chaplin, who in *City Lights* had pushed the stage-fright-struck ballerina out into the theater spotlight. I'd watched that film in my New York City apartment a few nights earlier, before setting sail for France. A week or so later, here I was, in Montparnasse as this beggar stopped, dug in his heels, and began to mouth smoke signals—indeed, "smoke" signals—directly in front of me, his eyes locked on mine. But a whole constellation now accumulated behind me. Was I tapping into an image pool? An image that lent itself to this scene? Yes, as I stared out through the window at that miming beggar beckoning, what distant images connected to this one? What was intercepting me?

A few blocks from the Dôme Café, at the Cimetière du Montparnasse, the poet Charles Baudelaire, in 1867, just forty-six years old, was buried. Likewise, Beauvoir and Sartre (in the same grave) and Samuel Beckett had their afterlife homes there. Not that I knew this. But seeping through the centuries, it seemed that a storage house (a café environment) of collective creative energy, a residue, a well of connectedness, dangled in front of me: a tantalizing, intangible key. As if authors before me, unclothed, divested of flesh, left behind their unused or unfinished inspiration. Or returned to the pool what they had taken, now modified. Returned an unconscious (to us) pool of images that played together in artists' imagination, never letting them go perhaps for their entire lives.

Obviously, when the desperate face of a gawky tramp glared into mine, *mimed* a request for a cigarette through a window of a café where Baudelaire had often sat—it was as if he flipped a switch. An epigenetics one—nonphysical? nontangible, subtle? This switch—in me—was to "Begin!" On some energy level (why not?), maybe there was genetics sequencing too, that could be "turned on." And so it was.

That signal, as if exiting a black hole, answered my request to Myself, my order to Write! Carried its lamp into the darkness—compelled, me to—that instant—draft page one of a novel (at least it began that way), *Love in Transition*, that took me thirty years to finish because it was the breeding ground of interceptions. Of nonhostile takeovers. This next signal came in 1985, in what I call the Zurich Initiation. It rebranded the "novel" as consciousness research, in disguise.

To this day, that 1965 signal tells me not to give up on *This* Book. To connect it back to the particles—of awareness, of consciousness—that sent it out, expecting birth.

This urgent instruction to start, this Alpha situation, is again at work. But it takes a consciousness seminar, remote, complete with assembled guides, to let me access those mighty collective energies that again, anew, renewed, push me, like in a *City Lights* shove. I balk. Am pushed further.

Now and then over the years, poems worked into my published prose. But I never gave the *poet me* center stage. Muffled, she mostly resided, tape over mouth, in boxes. Till a few years ago, clearing out cartons in my garage, weeding out the utter nonsense, I found poetry everywhere! The second-class citizen of me—this poet to whom words came easily because after all she was in the unconscious—revealed in those piles of papers just how prevalent she had been throughout my life, easily tossing off poems, whereas I, the prose writer, struggled, edited, cut, sweated, and finally was published. And published. But not she.

No longer is the poet stuffed in the closet. No longer are her messages unavailable. I see myself now at this late date as a custodian. A messenger.

For whoever is waiting for them, here they are, collected from 1985 (when they were in the future, bombarded into me from the spirit world) till 2021, definitively on par with this crazy year, joined right and left, watching/narrating as, at times, their predictions from then march into the material world, our Earth in crisis.

The only caveat I need to add is that some of this poetry has some lines too long to fit into a book-length line; this is especially true in "Encounters with Milton Klonsky after his death." Alas. They are quite long, as in *Leaves of Grass* or "Howl." Ginsberg explained that his long lines were meant to be read in one breath. Elsewhere, long lines have been called "oceanic."

Scenes in Hiding
They hide behind a brilliant white-out sun. Without blasting the sun into the
photo, the scenes were invisible. But an image composed of sunlight is hard put to go
through CMYK (four-color) book-printing, which dulls the colors outside its range.
Imagine treating sunlight like that.

1

Overview

The Whole of "It"

Encounters with Milton Klonsky
after his death

From the nothingness of thin air

My *Experience—no, vision—*of Reality

In meditation I saw
Milton Klonsky, now a spirit guide
a sudden looming apparition of himself pointed me to a
    spinning form
—I instantly knew what it was—
Dazzling, dangled in front of me,
A vision of "the Whole," the All—
Consciousness Itself

As if he made a scaled model of it

I watched in instant understanding
As he stepped out of flesh and blood into this meditation room
as if it were easy to make the transition
Appearing in my mind, my eyes shut,
Plucking essence from a Tree of Understanding
As if held out in his hand, Here it is
Satori

I saw

information moving as
a whole—it could not do otherwise, its nature seemingly—
bound together but not tightly;
shifting,
as it rippled through the All—
the fabric of it

precipitated by a
single insertion of movement—from anywhere—a single new fact

What in quantum mechanics language we deemed *irreversible*

As other options in the "cloud of possibility" in the particle realm
collapsed
and a unique event in time emerged—
was, to the whole,
the non-stand-still Unity,
recoverable.
It reorganized, in instant information-aware pieces
innumerable
throughout.
Inherent meaning kept moving, instantly "processed"—
juxtapositions in less than a split second acknowledged.
Or, let us say, the
quantum jumps of "information
units," "self-aware" (or "position-aware") feedback, or resonating
repositioning
Reshufflings.

Shift after shift,
Registered
Realigning,
As of an all-knowing—
or, all-Containing—transcendent consciousness
that did not have to "think," but merely to contain
Self-arranging, self-attracting information bits that excluded nothing
Aware of every move

now one, *now another* point, a new angle, was *energized by the whole.*

We screeched to a halt to invest in our reality as it cemented itself
    to us; feeling it definitive,
made concrete,
by a decision, an event.

If it was matter, it was
nailed down.

But every single
Perspective/point/information bit that existed, even potentially,
    could have *all information*
brought to bear behind it
if its turn came
AND it in turn *came forward*
—acting on *its* information,
its experience. Unconscious to us,

the whole had recalibrated with new information, absorbed and
digested it in what seemed to my physical eyes— no, my conscious-
ness—instantaneous. I watched as if looking at a UFO
the nonstop spinning of the All
in a nano-instant encompassing the ramifications in all directions
    of *any additional fact*
or event, reinforcing whichever centers of captured attention
now—

the wave function in quantum mechanics
describes all information
about the quantum state
But it is unpredictable what event it will favor among the "cloud" of
    congregating particles
The selection process is not up to
the particles in it (we think)

Rather, the "cloud" breaks,
and one, as it were, raindrop falls into, captures, our reality

But here I "saw" in great, massive dynamics
A veil removed so I could watch
Satori
that every new fact, event, bit of information spins with the All, in
the whole
as in a Vegas casino wheel,
without hesitation, without thought, without "time"

When we observe and collapse something—our "life"—out of
countless choices
the Whole absorbs that shift, that new status *of itself*,
And spins on, now different,
though with no discernible "stop."

In the perspective of the "whole," I saw—
the collapse is only
of "information." As if to a
non-time-bound level of Consciousness the outcome
in our 3-D world was a thought puzzle (*that could be rethought*).
Nothing was ever at a standstill there.
Anything in our matter world could regroup, reboot, wait for its turn
again, or leap into the new Now

I wondered, who/what was conscious
In this motion so fast
so "unthinking,"
or rather a calliope of invisible "thought"
become instant knowledge,
understanding, by association

I did not see the individual awareness
Just Awareness itself
Consciousness itself
Attached to no Aware-er per see
All
Aware
My delight, my joy, my astonishment

Scenes in Hiding detail

Here's What Got Me

Look, these laws of attraction based on size of mass and distance
between their centers

Spirituality concepts, **they** have Laws of Attraction too
but in no relationship to a law in physics, right?
Or gravity principles, are they in some way multidimensional
Is gravitational *attraction* multidimension
With layers of attraction as in a "forest of symbols"
How could that be?
It cannot
In 3-
D

Measurement Poems

A Communiqué

from my old mentor, Milton Klonsky,
a terse message out of "nowhere," again
in the nothingness of thin air

Starkly advising me to

"Measure Me"

proffering the suggestion

He meant it perplexingly, intriguingly,
—dangling just the mere idea—that his own energy (perish the thought)
  could be measured

Or asking me to tackle that conundrum of whether it could

He sent it telepathically:
Look, here's a good assignment. Look, I don't
need to spell it out. You see what I mean.

Okay. So you like to
Use a random number generator in your apartment. (Very much so.)
  But look.
I'm not here, physically speaking. Yet wouldn't you agree I'm very much
  here?
To find out how much, try to take a
measurement of me

my size, my dimensions.
My presence, location, speed,
Look at my composite interactions.

The message had popped in
on my mental screen, a screen
that didn't exist either.

As I stood in nature with my Belgian light body teacher in Ibiza, "jour-
   neying" with him in meditation
He led the way
And then suddenly my soul grouping was in my mind's eye in a U
   shape open ended
And Milton stepped forth from the group
With the question

I instantly saw the irony
I examined it up close, spellbound,
—turned it around—
To form yet another question.
Well, hmmm,

What if I measure *myself*

Look, *So here's a conundrum.*
"Can you—? Just envision it
Implicit was my preoccupation with a random number generator,
   trying to measure the energy in my apartment. But wasn't I thinking
   small?

The thought expanded

What if I measure *myself?*

Round the coastline of me several times over,
skidding and falling to the ground and getting back up and looking
    around
walking, taking the compass out, and the ruler, and the yardstick,
and the markers,
and whatnots, and finding that
this coastline of myself is irregular and also furthermore
it is shifting as I walk through it,
asking how to
MEASURE MYSELF

which locations *and which ways* a not totally
or rather not continually, not exclusively
physical—well, you see what it would take to get the hang of it.

Earlier, alive in a physical body, he had assigned me a different project,
    urgently, remember his own failings:
"Don't let *time* measure *you*. *You*
measure it."

So, Time too had me under a measuring rod

But wasn't this harder? The simple task, given from outer space—
real, warm, ironical, heart-challenging—
"Measure *me.*"

Of course, you, I, everyone had this task
not of finding out
who they were, but the implication would
exist—
that they were the one *there* and *there*
he had also once stated the principle to me
that space, time, AND PLOT,
given me that unique description: time/space

AND PLOT.
How could there be a space-time dimension
without plot?
So hold on, now. See what it turns into. Like a measuring
rod into personality, soul "size," presence,
energetic survival.
Not Planck lengths but the length of connections
as the threads wore thin or
strengthened.
Into—?

It implied or concluded: well, look, if the length of a fractal is
infinite, what about me?

Take my weight, that's easy
take my height and—well, let's not say depth—
take my width,
but suppose you ask instead to weigh,
to find the boundaries of—
myself

Where is my Plot-located energy?

Measure with the RNG?
Fine and well,

But while at it . . .
I flipped open the trans-dimensional cell phone
How do you measure a huge energy
Even a tiny energy, personified,
Calling it
"me"?

Rider on Horse Emerging
Scenes in Hiding detail (upside down)

2

A Dash of French

Gâteau Poems[1]
For the Earth, a "Cook-Key"

Written in 1986 in Zurich
With assistance from the Symbolic Mind, as word jingles pitch in
speaking to us, telling us how it
"Thinks,"
Not with the verbal brain,
It thinks in pictures; Baudelaire's prose poem of "Le Gateau" ("The Cake")"
started me off on this roller coaster,
Wham-bam
As the particles collided
chasing the transformations as the "cake" revealed itself to be a planetary "cook-
key," cooking up—?
for the Earth
the end of the twentieth century,
beginning of the twenty-first
all hands on deck!
here's a
Cook-Key
The syllables hit Attraction points
Wham-Bam
What was it typing?
Wham-Bam
Poems from The Christ State
Messages in poetry
A language mix-up

---

[1] *gâteau*—cake; pronounced "got tow"; *eau* is pronounced "O"; all French here and below

A Language Mix-up
Coin Flip
Toss-up

Energy
interconnected
stays
entangled
over infinite distance

in the particle world, deep down inside us and around us
that makes us up.
Does it now?
Make us up?

A mix-up,
a Tour de Force
a dangerous, daring plan

crossing language barriers

That should make a good setting
In the stratospheres of particles,
Of syllables at play

A
Come-
día

*

Was the *Last Supper* a
co-
may-dia
in mid-word, mid-syllable, a language shift

secret relationships—two, three languages—sliding in, safe, on base,
    in a single word
Just as if someone from Outer Space
shuffled a card deck there, so that,

comer—to eat—Spanish
co-*mère*[2]
spinning, dashing into each other,
what do you get?
A *comer* (to eat) Dia

Comedia.

Dante comes in: Hmmmmm. Perfect for the 21st century Let's call
    in Baudelaire.
Bringing
a nice birthday cake.
A *gâteau*.
Hmmm.
Now, everyone remember, bring your best gift for the new century,
Your most cherished
In donation to humanity
In donation to its unity, its Ground, its common Love
Lift Off

---

[2] *mère*—mother (Fr); *día*—day (Sp and Pt); co-may-*día*: *Divina Commedia*— *Divine Comedy*

Translations of the Cook-Key into English
Untangling the Entanglement

amare—to love (Lat)

arrêt—stop, halt (Fr)

atelier—artist's workshop, studio (Fr)

carte—map (Fr); book (Ro)

chaud—hot (Fr); pronounced "show"

ciel—sky (Fr); pron. "see L"; El—God (Hebrew, Phonecian, etc.); often at the end of prophets' names, as in Ezekiel

come— from *comer*, to eat (SP); pron. "co-may"; *dia*—day; Dante Alighieri's *Commedia*

complet—complete (FR); pron. "comb pleh" (come play)

don (Fr) = gift

en haut—on high (Fr); *haut* pron. "O" (*eau*/water—also pron. "O")

eté—summer (Fr); pron. "A tay"; rhymes with "Dan-te" and roughly "complet"; Mozart wrote "Longing for Spring" (January 1791), the year of his death; in *The Christ State*, this word play includes *printemps*—spring (Fr); *temps*—time, as in Print Time

Faust—fist (De)

four—oven (Fr)

hijo—baby, son, child (SP); Noli me tra—"Don't betray." After *Noli me tangere*—"don't touch me; I'm not yet in form" (Jesus to the Magdalene at the tomb)

oui—yes (Fr); pron. "we"

sentir—to feel (Fr)

triomphe—triumph (Fr)

Gâteau Poems

The Meta-4

I

So if we see the world as a Thought Form
the fourth dimension is a
meta4[3]
the oven where the cooking, the cake, was timed a
FOUR

Hold on now
A (French) four is . . . ? an (English) OVEN

A Cook-Key
is ready to come out in the open

a GOT TOW

Now what could be cooking
in a *meta*
Four. Turned On High
En Haut
in O
the *haut* in the end
not N-O now
En Haut[4]

A turned around spelling coming in
in
a
Meta-4

---

[3] *four*—oven; pronounced "foo-er"
[4] *en haut*—on high; *haut* is pronounced "O" (eau = water, also pron. "O")

II

Ready to go then
a New Era
here to Fore

God not
in the No anymore
The Littlest Plot
given volition

the most tiny
the wee Ours

Can we Trump-et an ending out of this?

For the Earth to go to a higher state
the karma had to be absorbed—
the lesson reversed

On one side he would be
of *the fenêtre*, window
hourglass
the signal *Now*: yes

for there was that certitude the *fenêtre* was
an *our*
glass

A Tour Nay
to turn no into yes

a courtship battle
in a
Tour
Nay

And now we learn the formula that will unbind
this web

Hologram Rhet finally
gotten beyond
as we go on with
Emily Brontë
out of
D-Quai

Is humankind ready then for this new turn?
—to step into the twenty-first century
and what is being stepped into?
—does it appear to be governed by?
High Comedy

An old signal
in the universe activated, to sense
sentir[5]

III

We on the Earth located our exploration outside
This project—located inside—was
digging into

[5] *sentir*—to feel

the true nature
of Man
in crisis position
where only one could survive
which one was the true one?
The Ego representative—
did that represent humankind?

Surely not—

A love that through centuries had been dwarfed
by the transcendent spirit
now the transcendent spirit
put all the strength behind the heart

In Terror gate
to ask of your Self in terror
in Terror
Gate
who am I?
Then do it
go through it
GATE O[6]

Once there was a woman who had two beautiful cookies
she put them under a spell and said
whatever happens
gâteaux say no

Got toe will travel

Got
toe
say
no

[6] Gate O—another form of *gâteau*; got tow

It must have something to do with a gate
Keeping him away from
a gate
—A Gate O
The *gâteaux*
who said no

And then someone said:
Take 2
GOT 2

At the reins
riding into the arena
In
formation
a chariot-
Tier

Ali-
Gate
Tor
GATE TOW
GATE-A Ω

IV

Will you marry me? asked the *oui* cell?
What? Marry the *oui*[7]
cell

---

[7] *oui*—yes; pron. "we"

He wanted
his Rites
demanded
she must give him
His Rites

The story that had never been told
The love story that had never been told
that slowly it can be told
the story of Jesus and
Mary Magdalene

and so he threw her thoughts into faraway orbit, where
they seemed to be having—if thoughts could have them—a fling
like the fastest birds, the swifts, who mate in the air
and throw themselves off a cliff or a nest,
these thoughts, as if they were javelins being thrown,
as far as the mightiest thrower could, seemed to be
having if thoughts could be said to
something like a fling.
In the depths of the archetype
there is almost no way
to deal with it
and an archetype one has oneself lived in
repeatedly

There was only emotion to deal with
massive amounts of emotion
accumulation
of emotion from over centuries
the whole treasure in it
the heart trans-
Plantation

Not to run
Not to run

this time
not to

V

In all those stories
what never got told

The seashell never
picked up
the one never heard sing
the one where the love story made its expression
the song sung now by
his soul
Nep-
TUNE

To plug into the energy of Jesus at a point where
something had never been said—
the seashell never picked up

the *Oui* Cell

The Littlest Plot
now we begin
to lift the lid

Scenes in Hiding detail

3

The FIRE Side (the Home Plot)
Jesus Poems

I heard a sentence: "Her water broke."

Instantly, I found myself before a council

(preceding my birth). I was asked *what* I "chose"

 "St. Paul." (without hesitation)

I watched

myself reply
What would I say?
No idea
No time to think
Just watch
Time stationary, fixed
Me a bystander
Then they said, "OK, but you also have to choose
Mary Magdalene"

Kundalini shaking up cellular blocks

the information trying to flow through newly unimpeded routes

Mary Magdalene

I know how I was born
what I came out of
I was the spark that wouldn't
that couldn't
go out

I wouldn't go out to be born
Yet neither would I
Nor COULD I
go out

The love story filled all the bookshelves
It entered all the libraries
of the spark that wouldn't
THAT couldn't go out

Embedding itself in the history of very intelligent men
having followed their brains
who buried their hearts

A Sublet

All this a secret enactment on the astral plane
all this totally unknown to the Earth
as the Exit of the Old Man began
as he with his helicopter tied around the Earth drew it to the next
   Stage
But his own story—that there underneath at the bottom deepest in
   his heart
the one that began
When Jesus looked down from the Cross
what dream was in his heart
Was it the New Year's Eve we did the town
Was it the one coming up on his horizon
Was it the one he forgot about
Was it that dream?
Did he
Reserve that dream
in his heart where no one would ever see it
till the negative was clearly finished
and the light ready to come on
to be turned on
how it developed in the dark through centuries
And this is it
the new development on that plot
that Jesus looking down on the Cross thought of
and got sustenance from
his love for
Mary Magdalene
D
I
D

All across the nation
a new vibration
ball in play now
this should be enough
for a real
PLAY
the kind he was good at
'cause oh my, how the boy can play
or we are such things as dreams ARE made
of that he now knew

The Old Man's Right to Privacy in His Own FIRE-side

I'd dreamed I would suddenly wake up
and my book be intercepted
But I didn't know that holding so firmly to my reins of the Truth
for myself I would wind up in this unconscious energy of the
Earth and all the things people never said
that would have made history go another way
I had no idea that if I did it well enough
if my heart was blown wide open
and my mind blown wide open
but in the end my heart
so that nothing else mattered
I would wind up in the Alternative Revelation
so deep it took centuries of master-hearting to get to it
a 2,000-year PLOT
by the boldest minds imaginable
but they found their hearts all this time
in being master minds
had got omitted

And they'd had that style of it enough
they would say their message from the heart
which she saw
looking at him so long ago
Miriam saw
and he said, "What would you, Miriam?"
and it stayed locked inside then
and stayed locked in
and history kept going one way
leading up to this way
when suddenly everything that was no turned into yes.

Imagine what an explosion that would be
and so it exploded in me
the answer to the question
that was his own vibration
and was coded into the DNAs of his and her personalities
that if ever the day came
the question was presented again
and it happened by the way to be coded to a personal
apocalypse
that would snowball,

well, just look what the real answer was

practically saying there will be no 21st century
if the King stepped down
dethroned himself
for what was that crown
if he couldn't share
couldn't have a heart like other men

In lesson form
the lessons they had learned
HIS HAND
THE OLD MAN'S
when he reveals it

As he's opening my hand now
the hand I didn't know I had
that I was one of those who agreed and even shouted that I
wanted to do this
help bring in the Real RITES OF MAN
starting with the rites of his own FIRE SIDE
the Old Man's privacy in his own FIRE SIDE

he had never been allowed that
because where could he get protection enough
it didn't exist
how to protect
A VIBRATION LIKE THIS
his own when he looked at Mary Magdalene
just as he had on the Cross
and then he'd get strength from her

My computer when I felt the question and wrote it wrote the
answer
as the power behind it is fueling everything written here

D
I
D

Lessons for the Earth in its changing position
now what use for a
medium
THE MEDIUM
OF
LOVE

LOVE
IN
TRANSITION
THE MEDIUM
Of LOVE

For it was in the air now
the germ of it all
the real story behind

The American Dream
in this version
The real one
A
MARY
CAN

WHEN SHE SAID, "I CAN"
and shouted it so loud her personalities heard it
and his heard too
and thus the Avenue being walked down by Christ and Mary
Magdalene
AT THE END OF THE CENTURY
was not the Unthinkable one
in the predictions
for they were set to counteract those predictions
thus it was something long in preparation was coming into
being and it was meant to be Peace on Earth
but the Alternative would be rampaging war the like of which
had never been seen
if when he opened his heart and said I love you
the world unthinkingly picked it up
picked his vibration up
his private vibration
invisible though it was
....

"His mouth was like the heart of a POMegranate"—
Gibran said
Mary Magdalene thought then
keeping quiet about how she felt

But this Avenue being walked down by Christ and Mary
Magdalene
opened to the Arc de Tri-OMP-he[8]
and all that was behind that Tree
a circle surrounding the explosion of his light
when the Old Man told the new man
what was going on

As entities had moved into the orbit of the Earth
to bring to the Earth
in transformation stories they themselves and others had made
to reach their new State
lessons for the Earth in its changing position
now what use for a medium:
the Medium
OF LOVE

Love in Transition
in the medium of Love

[8] the fifty-meters high Arch of Triumph at Place de l'Étoile, Champs-Élysées, Paris

4

Atelier
Dante

Concavities
Inward curving
introspective
Notions
Jumping in to
Facilitate
Our introspection

The second stanza should begin with "and"

I woke
the words ringing in my ears

"The second stanza should begin with AND"

Connect
Connect
An-
dante

Atelier Dante

the Earth barreling toward the twenty-first century,
with most of the inhabitants unaware of the challenges it would face
raced toward

At the computer
COMMAND
DANTE

Watching the screen
cheering us on
a TELLY YAY[9]
a Telly Yay

A desire to vacuum the Earth
to restore its beauty
to value what had seemed insignificant
had no place
the idea penetrating
that without this sense of life
life was not worth living
and more it would disappear

[9] An atelier, or workshop, is roughly pronounced (Fr) "a telly yah"

This a message from the future
just as Robert had received a message
from his future self
telling him to
self-destruct
telling now the inhabitants of the Earth
to self-destruct
from their present path
get off that path

In the room in Zurich I paced and the thoughts came into my head, the song tunes accompanying, the excitement riveting, as *The Christ State* flowed into me. A newspaper was being published from Outer Space. Not a spacecraft landing, but thoughts coming in, into my head, into the stratosphere, thoughts of a planetary shift. 1985.

Face Materliazing
detail

To the Earth

I

Extra, extra, read all about it—
the End of the World
everywhere, alarms were going off,
people waking up
waiting for this signal
the end of the world
waiting to bring it about
the end of the world

Robert died.
It was the end of the world.

People waking up
inner alarms going off
rung from the astral plane
A man on the astral plane
clanging the dinner bell
saying there was food for the masses
come to the gathering
meet here to dine
That the food long in preparation was ready
that there was sole for breakfast
As in the biblical days
make from one fish food for everyone
For the New Age breakfast was ready
And the breakfast of the New Age
was the sole of Man

The breakfast of the New Age was being prepared
Now everything fell into place
Alarms sounding
people waking up
understanding the inner ringing
Hearing it in their sleep
from a clock
that was invisible
Audible this sound
from high up in the astral plane
calling Man to wake up
that a truck was driving to his/her door this very minute
a delivery being made
a green truck
a spring truck
it was
under way
the leap into the New Age

Cymbals clanging and a happy dance
for its ready at last
slimmed down
completely prepared
The sole of Man/Womankind
is ready.

Outwardly a chaotic scene
a world nearing doomsday, to some appearance,
but inwardly the long-awaited moment
the chance of ages
the buildup of thousands of years
for the outer disturbance
is a mirror

something seen from across a window
a window into Man's soul
and in that soul the end of the world is a blessing
an age is being carried out.
People waking up
inner alarm ringing
ringing in
the New Age

And then the overall structure became clear
there was clarity
there was a plot behind the apparent plot
news to be published
there was a *New York Times* edition to get out
how the sun set on the *New York Times* building
and after setting in brilliant gold
became a human head
and that after moments turned into cartoon figures
a comic strip in the air
a punchline after all
animals in cartoon scenes
there was the human story there
there was the larger purpose becoming visible

for the breakfast of the New Age
was being prepared
utter calm
but something serious was in the air—
Death being dislodged

it wasn't the expected turn
the return of Robert
as Ulysses this time

to tell the story of
why death was being dislodged
he had seen it
the second hand now seen for what it was
Man was getting the story secondhand

living a version that was secondhand
but a revision had been sent
the manuscript as it really was
the script for Man
the blueprint
the Uman script
and not the secondhand
but first-
hand

He had gotten the thread
the thread that tied up the past
this was not the Old Man
was a totally New Man
the missing link

For the cancer had only been for purpose of re-
mission
this death and many other deaths
something tremendous was in the air
as the past became clarified
Man at a rhet-
Turn
a revelation under way
a modern Gospel
the prophetic line of humanity
reaching the point of its leap of faith

The whole human race taking a leap together?
Yes, the whole human race
leaping out of
the end of the world
finding there was an alternative to the
end of the world

There was a new plan.

II

We know all about the established Tradition
but did any of us here know about the X-
TRADITION

But how is it possible that Life was extradited
right under man's nose
and we didn't do a thing
took our own life away
and we didn't do a thing
for knowing nothing about it
knew nothing at all about this practice of X-
Tradition

For the Last Supper
the first time
was—he now saw—was
completely convinced—leading to
A *Come-Dia*[10]
Sole for Breakfast

In springtime
Man in springtime

given
A blue-
Print
the trump
ET

Mozart his last SPRING
springTIME
in
E-
té

For we have two Christs here
one who stopped
and one would join him
in
E-
té[11]

You've never played with me
Com-
Plet[12]
End of the world
suddenly what do we see
Pier-
O[13]

The call to Man had come
The telephone rang

[10] come—eat (Sp); pronounced "co-may"; dia—day (Sp); Dante's *Commedia*
[11] *été*—summer; pron. "a-tay"; rhymes with "Dan-te" and roughly "complet." Mozart wrote
"Longing for Springtime" (1791) just before his birthday; he died December 5; word play in
The Christ State includes *printemps*—spring (Fr); *temps*—time, as in Print Time
[12] complet—complete (Fr); pron. "comb play"

It was Christ on the line
He was calling Man as in the biblical days
rounding up followers
asking who was with him. Who against
which of us would make this jump into the
twenty-first century
the telephone to the earth rang
it was Christ calling

Many were ready for the new image
many suspected the old image
were ready for the radical transformation
the conversion
to the potential of Woman/Man
would hear in their heart
the reverberating answer
that they were not the Old, but the
New Woman/Man

The road was complete
though the pavement had not yet hardened
He himself
had already traveled the whole path
Aa new Way had opened:
—the sign in the road

There was a Way open:
CLOSED
DEATH AFTER LIFE

---

¹³ Pierrot—pron "pier row," a clown

At this point a barrier is reached
the material beyond it brand-new
the announcement of the New Age is received
Planted clearly visible
Rising starkly
a gift of God to humanity
that at the closing
of this age
a new closing is taking place

The signpost in big letters
there's nothing small about this
and there's no fine print
it's an unambiguous New Way.

IV

Now the cry is being given
the signal sounded
to rescue the Earth

but this would take strong leadership
this would take a sacrifice
this would take a death

the man at the head of the Old Line
would have to make a break in tradition
would have to create a passage where there was none

There was a tunnel the female was led through
by her mother
with little animals on the walls

alive but unmoving
—led safely all the way through

V

Christ as a person
as even his intimates
never knew him

The jump onto the ledge to get his diaries
explosion of the spiritual bomb
Man finding his heart wants to speak
wants to follow this path too
secretly loved the Earth too
realizing that a crossroads has come
a turning point
a moment of decision
Is he capable of this sacrifice?
Is the male capable of stopping?
Is the male capable of standing
behind the female
to save
the Earth?

For the train home is on a high track
there's no possibility of arriving
except on this track
the train of associations following
a very high track
the lower associations left behind
Man following the higher associations

the higher picture of female
an image of the intuited strength of female
Man putting his reputation into the hand of female
sure she has this strength
will stake his life on it
he will leave his inheritance to her
and on her decisions his whole
inheritance ride
Man putting trust where it was withheld
ignoring signs to the contrary
following the other track
the signs of optimism
he knows her capability
he accepts her
Man following
the female

Now that the way had been cleared
we did not have to die
physically, in moments of great, taxing change
but to go beyond the known boundaries of this world
beyond the ego boundaries
the boundaries long protected by the ego
go exploring into unknown space

What he said before was for the masses
what he says this time
is for the individual

VI

Here then is the extra edition
the extra edition
of the Earth as
a planet among other planets
as the name it's known by
as Planet Earth
the Earth as a youngster
a physical-energy child
not knowing what to do with her energy
she had so much
the Earth as a maverick
in the grouping of planets
revolving around
the sun

VII

A young man now has the preparation ready

In celebration
in jubilation
Co-may-
Dia

A view of the world
from a high perspective
Come-
Dia

Mozart knew well

the Square dance of life
he very much intends to teach
That the story
of our *Commedia*
Mozart at the helm
for a course on
Life

VIII

In 1492 the Genoese
Cristóbal Colón
set sail from Spain
looking for a shortcut to the East
to make a trade route to the East
the land of spices
set said looking for the connection
some link, some opening
to shorten the distance
a direct route
some body of water

All he found, though
was two continents full of gold
of aborigine people

Began the Colonial period
when it was really something in Man
meant to be COLONized
given the
equality symbol
The breakthrough

passageway
arrived at indirectly
he sought
directly
geographically
between East and West
de-
colonization
of the inner Man

IX

The whole ball of yarn
the yarn of the Second Coming
unfolding now in two directions
Man being told so we can take control of it
else this unfolding lead at flying speed
to the atomic war we don't want
that line crossed that would initiate it unless halted and leading
   also to
the message of this book

For when the ego crosses the line of death
the result is death
only the Self can cross
the line of death conscious

the multitude of times it will come
the individual day of Judgment
we don't have to do it physically
it's our egos who die, transform crossing it

for this is the line the shadow drew
the line separating the Old World from the New

The intensity needed to make possible
the greater consciousness
carries with it
the alternative of creating an enormously
Heightened
Unconsciousness

—all that is potentially conscious
now,
through this gift,
also potentially unconscious
That great an energy field
received unconsciously
would create an ego drive
in unparallel form
the Anti-Christ
the Anti-World
the opposite choice

an emotional state
with no clue as to its real purpose
feeling however the sense of purpose
yet totally unconscious as to the deeper, broader
purpose
There had to be
the energy of God
energizing
saving the Earth
and the energy of God
turned wrong

in the name of God
works divisiveness
—however carrying with it a magnetism

We are facing the choice of letting
the ego use
this tremendous emotional energy
as Hitler did
and then we would have chosen—yes, we—the
anti-Christ

by nothing more than tapping into
the archetypal energy field
of the Christ consciousness
like a pirate
to a radio station
—this done by the ego
reaches other egos
And what is meant to be used
for transcendent purposes
is used
selfishly
—all that is Christ unconscious
yet the furor of sense of mission
picked up
and magnetically transferred into a field
that has followers
thinking they follow
one who truly knows

In trying to save the Earth
the current is put

intensified
around the Earth
of both possibilities
—for it's in the form of consciousness

The End of the World as the Return unto God
is in the air
to Source, Spirit, Creator, Knowing, Unity . . .
but in order to put the salvation story into
the current surrounding the Earth
coming toward the Earth
the form had to be one of choice
We're in a tremendous energy field
of the Return to God
the Return Home
but those same forces
misunderstood
would lead to
the other end
of the world
it's up to us to choose
and there's no way out
of the choice
for we're in the midst of the motif
the forces of it
the energy of it
the End of the World

And God in return is brainstorming Man
toward the other end
but so long as
the mind is unfree

we're likely to misread the meaning of the forces felt
think they mean a personal gift

There is an attempt now to raise
the whole Earth to the level
that can master
physical energy
Many people have to regress to come to the Earth and be put
under the laws of physical energy
for they already know these laws
and have a leashed power
within
them
an unsuspected power
within them

Robert as St. John
announcing the Revelation
announcing the gift of the salvation of Man
or the refusal of the GIFT

of the salvation
of Man
of Arma-
ged-
DON[14]

[14]don—gift (Fr)

5

FIRE Side Poetry (cont'd)

A Good SHOW

And God said
this should make a
Good
chaud[15]

The Home Plot
the Fire Side of Man
out of the
Shad-dough

One side of the Earth in Light
the dark side in shadow
the two harmonizing together
look around and see it is so

Find the scent brand new of
the twenty-first century
at
traction

A GOOD *CHAUD*
God said
a
really good
chaud
fire
side
of the

[15] *chaud*—hot (Fr); pronounced "show"

Light
energy
Giving it to the Old Earth at the crossroads
standing in the center of the road as the earth
lumbered along
into the undesirable future of straight-ahead
picking the entire Earth belief system up on a finger
redirecting the straight-ahead direction

Signal *ARRÊTE!*[16]
STOP!
ARRÊTE!
stop
stop, Earth

Cig-
ARRET
garret of the signal carriers to STOP

The *FOUR* time reached[17]
in the oveN
where the cooking went on
the radiation went forth
held in a central holding system
the *cook*-key

Irony so amplified
paradox so multiplied
all loopholes to escape so eliminated
a consciousness so elaborate there was no way to get around it
mind

[16] *arrêt*—stop (Fr); pronounced "a Rhet"
[17] *four*—oven (Fr); pron. "foo-er"

and
fore-
thought
gate open
Leaving the Old Earth
leaving behind some of their energy
masters of the past
project's finish

Dot dot Dash dot
dash dash dash
Morse code into my ears, my
unconscious ears,
taking us into the
next century

And in each V a group of faces
just as I as a tiny tot saw in a preview
at the card table

That child's-eye view as I, who went down the stairs into the living room,
witnessed the symbolic action years ahead
how the game of my life
as above so below
an archetype of the century
was to be played
peering long into the future
the day that a winning hand
hand full of cards
would be in
sky
formation
This is Crew

C-
El
see El
from the Cells
ciel[18]

Come in, Earth
This is
CREW CIEL

deeply believing that the Earth is ready for such an opportunity
Singing into the atmosphere

SAVE
THIS PLANET
the mountain of commitment
this is it

THAT MOUNTAIN

For a truth
from origins beyond the Earth
that until now had not been able
to
now has
Ulysses' love had
PENNY-
TRATED

[18]*ciel*—sky (Fr); pron. "see L'; El—God (Hebrew, Phoenician, etc.); often at the end of prophets' names, as in Ezekiel; "ah" is similar.

6

RUMI-NATIONS

Cells and the Soul

Kill the cell
Consciousness
Moves to another
Cell—
Or no cell
No mind

Oh, but I feel alone
(the personality)
how could *you* be so brave?
Risking me?
(My personality
—to the soul)
—brazen of you to think I could be so courageous

Where did you voyage from, my soul?
Before you were me—
Just
Consciousness
Perhaps of someone else?!
Became me
Quantizing
Consciousness
It's why I feel scared sometimes
Imagining myself as

Quantized
Consciousness

But it's fun, it's fun,
Said the soul
Follow me
And so I took my first out-of-body trip, following
her, to I never found out where,
the
Little Ball of
Quantized
Love
Quantized
Wisdom
Quantized
Into Me

In a Vision She Came

It wasn't a shock to me,
I expected it
To lose my virginity that night
But lo! She came over my head
My first image of That Me,
wise, it was clear,
larger, beckoning me to follow
out of my body, go with her
And I did

A compression of reality
I didn't know of
Over my head
In the shape of/Ball of a giant particle
Form of
At least
I think it's true
ME
Poised over my head I could see
As down below, where I was, another initiation was setting itself up
I was eager
Ready to lose my virginity
But oh no, she had another destination, come follow out of my body
As my body got ready below
by itself she said leave it
let it handle the experience alone

A ball of my consciousness
Before I received it
She much more settled into the wider universe

I then knew little of
My consciousness
Out of My body
alive and beckoning
My soul aware, beckoning me

Feeling Alone

My dog has panic attacks when I leave
As if part of himself is gone
Perhaps that's it
Perhaps it's not a memory
Of being hit on the back end as a puppy
Or "the abandonment syndrome"
of dachshunds
Especially as he, the only other living being in the room, saw his
first human mother die
No,
Perhaps I'm, in his mind, his connection to the love in the universe
Without it he feels thrown out
Just as when I in a sudden moment feel I've lost my connection
with the universe
disconnected from it
I feel afraid, have to get it back

So perhaps it's not just something he invented
Or dogs together invented
Perhaps, specifically, he's in my energy
Feeling, on his level,
that when I leave it's as if the universe
Specifically the love in the universe
has left him adrift
love which makes all things right
Perhaps he's feeling the Pattern
Yes, the pattern
In part "catching" it from me
Ah ha
I see

Hard to communicate the point but
Sometimes at night in bed I feel scared,
Then I realize I've fallen out of my connection with the universe,
Then I might reach for him, feel his warmth, and I'm connected again
in the warmth, the beating life force

It's the connection flowing through all of us, all life, that perhaps
needs love to carry it
Then in that instant, be connected again

I remember when my father died
That last instant
He looked us all in the eye, round once
Then
The circle twice
He said, *Hold my hand*
Why? Was it just on the 3-D level
Well, more deeply elementary I now see

The hand held the warmth of connection
But not just personal
We all carried
The Love in the universe
for him, connected to him
The love of the All for him in one package in each of us individually
As the world turned in love of him
As we held it in our eyes
Grasping for that last human chance
Connecting him into the universe
Into those that went before through this moment
Into us staying behind,
Into memoires
Carried in that touch,

And when he went into a coma we asked *if you can still hear us*
Squeeze our hand.
With great effort—how much?—a dying act, he did.
Where there was almost no life left here, his spark of life, his last
energy marshalled every particle of him to
Squeeze
Our
Hand

That hand that had held ours remained warm,
Unable to speak but yes, to hear, paralyzed, still he squeezed
And then I noticed in the casket
That one hand
felt just barely

warm
Leaving a sign behind
Love demonstrating it endured

Flowing through us, calling on the universe to help us express it
The Love

Mystical Writings

I

Memories steered through
bypassed when need be
memories that were all we had
you and me
ways I will recognize you
don't tell me how
let me
let me
I want to
tell you

II

Music notes in the flying plane
only music notes for bars
counterpoint unusual
soul flying among the stars

To go and
or not to go
to be and
or
not to

Too big to be
one symphony
and yet—
and yet—

Two forms of you
wordless, silent, speak
your words mute, heart-communicated
you
trapped
and not trapped
pressing the meaning into me
compressed into the meaning
between us
One symphony heard in the plane
you inside
you showed me
struggling to stay in that size when you
were that so many places
you identified with the size of the music
the notes barring a change to larger
and yet, and yet—
the struggle of size still contained in the way
you showed me you were there
in the bars of the music
everyone in the plane
might play

how explain to another this bigness of form, this form
how explain a form
not possible here
Not possible?
well, not thought to be possible

and yet, and yet—

I felt it
your soul struggling in the bars
not to be free, but that the two forms coincided
the music
full inspiration as could be
yet it was the music itself you were in, not in person
and yet, and yet—
saying large as I am—
feel me in the struggle—
aware and not in an aware form
unless is the music note aware
but you held the notes into a symphony trembling
to stay there and not at once
the music
notes in the flying plane
in the universe that can be music abstractly if it wants to
and yet, and yet—
remembering and therefore still
the entity consciousness
commitment
not lost, not turned away from
therefore
communication possible
all the feeling received

What would love do?
accept that this was you
Led, entering into your dreams at night
to wake you up
but you are awake
it would seem

in your universe
but not in mine and so
I tell you so
in your dreams
and then you do in fact
wake
counterpoint unusual
universe to universe

III

Who was the messenger? What the message
sent in that cylinder down that dark corridor
you
folded into
I called the past?

IV

The dam that had separated us emotionally from God
from that energy—in the Garden
abused sexually
—and because of which He/She hid his heart—
Now that we had developed the GodHEAD further
and made no effort to find that heart
to find him
had said we knew He existed
and then made up an old man with a beard
on a throne

hadn't imagined a living energy

Had seen he could if he would
overturn the tables in the temple
and as Samson
overturn the Whole Temple
but that He refrained
He has kept leashed and chained—

V

Guides adding Dim-
MENTIONS
information
and what they started with in this
Un-
earthing
was this powerful message from Pluto
That it wasn't just a planet
at a great distance from the Earth but something with a message
for
now

How often they had been seen and not heard
been herd
guides adding dim-
mentions
reality of
the Earth position

VI

But what could do it
cause a child who had worked toward sleep
to reject the sleep
because coming with it
was paralysis
lying in bed
unable to move
only the mind awake

To think with the mind
the mind above the physical distress
high above and still functioning
talking to the panicked emotions
lying in bed between waking and sleeping
then the mind taking over
with pure mind it could do it
talk the body
into waking up

VII

We're all of adventurous spirit
we're all in our Viking ships here
we're all ready for a new world here
we'd all love a new world just to appear
in the unconscious ocean
we'd love to look out one day from the prow of the ship

and look there it is—
look, there it is
it's land near
Then all we want is to go to it
we want to believe in it
the world that supplanted the old fallen leaf
the old C-
leaf
the new B-
Leaf
Just like the central door in a quantum probability theorem
we'll walk through
when we walk through this door
when we see land
We walk through the AIR PORTE
this is the door—this is the door to it
and we all turn over our leaves
here's a very new leaf—
it's not the old leaf at all
it's a BE-
LEIF for us all

Shut-In

Once there was a little girl whom no one told to shut up
but they told to "Take this button in your mouth and—"
and it all went well till the insides
closed the N
shut all the air out
and then she would be shut up,
except that she learned how to
live as a shut
N

The Descartes We Never Hear About

Concerning the objects presented to us we should investigate, not what others have thought nor what we ourselves conjecture, but what we can intuit clearly and evidently or deduce with certainty, since knowledge is acquired by no other means.

—René Descartes

In the universe, there are things that are known, and things that are unknown, and in between there are doors.

—Paraphrase from The Doors

Menu
carte[19]
À la carte?
before the
horse?
Not before the horse

Back to
DAY
CARTES

Tearing everything down

Do it
he said, once in a lifetime, start from scratch

[19] *carte*—map (Fr); book (Ro)

Everything must be
Torn down,

Razed,
bulldozed,
the blueprint shredded
assumptions be gone,
de-
molished

7

*Twenty-first Century
(Mostly)*

After Whitman

On contemplating: I am part and parcel of all that I survey

I AM

Part and parcel of

. . . the grids and bridges of me,
the optical ILLUSIONS
of me
the feeling inside the rhythms of this as truth
part and particle of the warps of me
the cascading or retaining or releasing spills and quark oceans of the
    implications of me
the infinity of the past of me and
the future of the many directions of those
options of me
the virtuosos of nano shapes of me, the powerful combinations, the
    forceful decisiveness, the
        dematerializing dimension of the creative energies of me, the
        neutrinos that pass through en route perhaps to the center of the
        Earth or coming from there and through,
AS ARE YOU

—surveying HOW?

Jobless, Eyeless Pixels

Reason, or the ratio of all we have already known, is not the same
that it shall be when we know more.

This life's dim windows of the soul
Distorts the Heavens from pole to pole,
And leads you to believe a lie
When you see with, not through, the eye.

—Blake

I see WITH the eye
I don't see the trees, but the detection of the trees
I don't even smell them, I smell the *patterns* of the smell, I translate
inside preconditioning

So we pick this up; that we want to escape the patterns inside
the eyeless pixels, the news reports, the habits we step into
—all energized on the quantum level
till we "see" something in them, "read" something in them,
and the unity
collapses.

I don't see a leaf, I see the pattern of a leaf

and then one day it all changed
I SEE the leaf, it shimmers, dancing,
as to Van Gogh

Thus,
these clouds as I stare up meditatively at long stretches
spellbind me
in nonconditioned patterning
I am the actuality
if I can throw off the shackles, expect the unexpected
I can do this, not see in the small patterns that fear introduces.
I can be free

This I woke to, to pass on quickly, hurriedly, a message from Love and
Freed-Om

Connectedness

How to be You: Claim It

But do you have that right?
In places where you are different, perhaps "ahead"
—surely ahead, a little voice says,
Admit it, don't be shy, don't be bashful

How can you claim that part of yourself
Or suppose someone else is speaking your ideas
How can you, even so, claim yourself as you?

Impotence—Stripped, Flayed

People can
strip you of all existence
take over your
Energy field—
because you threw up your hands, gave it away—
the Energy
barreling
emptying
draining out of you
went toward the New Center—

That's okay

If it fitted the situation
No sweat, no problem
but not if you remain in
Your erased you
A now-empty field of potential
overshadowed
by the claim you forgot to make on it
to incarnate it,
inhabit it

but I never learned how, you say
Oh no?

never suspected you had the right
which would exist only after you stepped into it—could
feel it inside

Do not, as you so often did, leave
your deep Energy—
swallowed up now, in a field with no
apparent connection to you
—no discernible relationship
because
your Energy is
imprisoned, speechless on your behalf
dis-
placed.

5-D, 10-D

I saw
Mother Mary
with a basket overhead flying
Once in the 1990s

Overhead then, decades after I perhaps saw her—was it so?— as a
    Little Dot I followed three decades earlier,

I saw her
flying
but I was flying with her
this time clearly visible
it was me

an angelic sight, a vision clear as day
in my meditation

Over her arm was this basket she reached into, as to get flowers and
    sprinkle them down the aisle at a wedding,
Whatever was inside floated down,
as she handed out
as-if-petals

beckoning me
magically
to join in the distributing
As I watched
I did.

But what about my hard-fought-to-find creations
I'd always protected, feared to lose
working solitarily, throwing a coat or other camouflage over them
so no one could see while they slept
me and Creativity solitarily at work
copyrighted every one,

but in that moment
unhesitating
As I watched
I saw Mother Mary up there with her basket, me at her side,
dip my hand into the basket,
pulling out, distributing
Watching, I knew that in the basket might well be,
must be, I thought, parts of my creations, of "me,"
what I "owned,"
But I smiled, why?

As I watched myself, my 5-D or 10-D self, without a thought to any
    objection,
Blended, magically blissful
Distributing the blessing
in there with other
indicators of
connectedness

All forgotten in an instant
of being beckoned to join in as she distributed.

How indelible the moment was
I watched, cheering her and myself on in silence, as a part of me
flying with Mother Mary
dipped into her basket of blessings
distributing.

We are One, her basket said to me.
part of a Universal Energy,
This is more complicated than you can understand right now
But your instinct is superb
It's just right

As patterns she'd had cleared to a point could be
picked up at that point, taken further

if you reached energetically,
resonating with, asked for
trusting to receive
from her basket of
anonymous blessings.

And was this she who, decades earlier, as the Little Dot took me on a journey I forgot? I think so. Then it was pure consciousness with no incarnation seen. Above, for a split second, I was allowed to see her and myself at her side

Yet a couple more decades later, 2021, I made a click. I sat at the computer, working not on my own writings but editing. In a barrage of requests. Super-inundated. Why? And why did it make me smile? Why do the solutions flood my fingertips? Suddenly I catch the smile I had, watching my 10-D self distribute as I below marveled, and the smile I have now, watching me meet with no problem the barrage of editing requests.

Distributing. The same smile, same frequency. Up there high above, reaching into her consciousness, her basket of energetic petals

Distributing.

8

Remembering Hunter Thompson (mostly)

People need trouble—a little frustration to sharpen the spirit on, toughen it. Artists do; I don't mean you need to live in a rat hole or gutter, but you have to learn fortitude, endurance. Only vegetables are happy.

—William Faulkner

A Poet

Break into my house
break my arm
break my leg
now and then
break your word
even that
but never
BREAK
My
CON-
CENTRATION

Break the table,
break the cha-
ir
break
the Olympic record
I don't care
but don't
BR-
EAK
My
Concen-
tration
Break my wrist
No, not my neck
but don't ever break in when
I'm in
my
concentration

You react in
self-defense when
someone beats and attacks you severely
but how can I explain
it's just the same
if
you break in
on me when
I'm in
my
concentration

A Tribute

He put on a hat
I thought: *I might like to wear a hat*
Would it look outrageous?
—out of place?
—silly?
He said
go ahead.

He didn't seem to weigh
all of those questions
he didn't care
he didn't say it looked
good or bad
he said
Go ahead.

If I wanted to,
go ahead.

Hunter

I woke with this thought
the first line
the words were unspecific
the idea was there
the idea didn't shift

He was wearing a hat
he didn't need my permission or approval
he put it on

all these thoughts darted to check my impulse
he didn't check my impulse
he put it front and center
if I wanted to
he wanted me to
so he said
without the rest of the words
go ahead.

I didn't usually wear a hat
it was a sudden impulse

I had a crazy cowboy one
and a cute flat one
whichever I reached for
he didn't blink
or think twice about it
just go for it

If that's what you want
the world out there,
it won't bite
I won't
if you want to,
go ahead.

He said Duke helped him talk crazy
Yet that wasn't the way
he saw the hat deal
in my case
forget about the alter ego
just if you want to,
I'll back you up.

Hunter.

As my brother-in-law told me, reading about him in 2005
in all the papers, "I think there's a little bit of Hunter Thompson in
   all of us."
And I say, he said,

if you want to,
go ahead.

A Visit to Owl Farm in 1991

I needed to see the twenty-odd-years-later Hunter
rekindle that fire, watch him in his now-famous attire,
and so we close on that:

My voyage with
an old alchemist's key
to decipher here
what it really means
when the mate to Faust turns out to be
the one voyaging with
MEFIST
O

When Goethe said,
"his fist,"
he said,
seine Faust[20]

---

[20]*Faust*—fist (De); Hunter is associated with the famous Gonzo fist.

A logo, forest of symbols
A fist

Electricity Baths

I gathered up my Tibetan conch, thinking of Joska Soos de Sovar,
    Hungarian shaman
he bought it in London from fleeing Tibetan monks
the old ceremonial conch

Gathered up also my sacred Sanskrit conch, bought at an Ibiza flea
    market, and drove
to the Watersong Peace Chamber just
outside Pittsboro.
an initiation

Native American
shamanic healing-sound workshop
led by Kailash Kokopelli,
playing
Didgeridoo (Native
American) flutes, reed instruments, drums, singing bowls
A pioneer sound therapist

Joska had written *I Do Not Heal, I Restore Harmony*
he spoke of "traveling without moving,"
said distance didn't exist (didn't have to).

I handed the instruments to Kailash

eyes closed

hearing only the indigenous-instrument sounds made by Kailash
in the group meditation
I had
this physical sensation
the pure, blissful, visceral, awareness—
of the delicacy of sensuality
experiencing the sensation of the cells . . .
Felt the prickles, the bristling sensitivity
the movement so miniscule
phenomenal

Feeling inside me the sensation travel, identifying the
path
the rivulets of light wound, wavy, as they surfed, shot through me
peaked, exploded
vibrating in pure sensation, there awoke in me
this overwhelming sense of the holiness of
the mere trace of
a touch—or subtle touch—on the skin,
so holy, this body
we live in

how the cells feel that subtle sacredness:
light meeting light;
utter sensuality at the merest encounter.
Of the purity of sensuality
a human condition we mostly don't know,
as Joy tingles. Something
in the archetype of the feminine
(and the masculine) at its most awakened. I remembered the Magdalena
    described as being
"*very* sensual and *very* pure"

as the particle level contact crossed into expression—feeling—in
    matter,
in my body.

Nothing is solid.
sitting in your chair, you're
100-millionth of a centimeter above it; you are not touching it but
sensing the atomic repulsion between its atoms and yours.

At home in guided meditations mornings

I continued to feel the exploding rivulets of light. Rivulets traveling
Downstream, upstream and then peaking
Atomic
repulsion? Energizing me in bed before getting up to
work on "The Hunter Thompson Story"
for two or three years.

Sometimes I closed
my eyes and saw this indescribable, fast-moving geometric energy,
gone so fast my brain barely had time to register—
zero time to get descriptive words. An "aerial phenomenon," a UFO.
    Only, inside. Not out-. But something in me gasped,

what just went past?
like a chunk of rock or a meteor, black-bluish, lumpy, brilliant
no
rays, twinkling without light.
cosmic bullet in another
dimension my brain in sync with less than
a split second
that part of us aware before the brain, before thought gets the news

long enough
to let me see it and smile. Stay, don't go. Show me more.
I loved the fact that it might show up at any time. Here. Gone.
Zoom. Swoosh. Hot damn. Kazaar.

The Dots—Do They Connect?

Dream or Vision?

Time to go
Leave Europe
Leave Belgium
the dream told me
Go to U.S.
Why?

Something is going on over there
You're to help with it

Help write "The Hunter Thompson Story"

I told Hunter the dream
Reminded him in a letter

Did he register it?

Life purpose
Death purpose
Alpha Omega
Again
Got Tow
Gâteau
Crew
See
El

Cake
Frosting on

Death plan?
Dream or vision?

Event Ball?

I lie in bed
Nearby the car crash is occurring
I see myself in the dream pack up and go to the U.S. to help write
   The Hunter Thompson Story

Dream or prophecy—
What
is an event ball?
A word I made up
Dream
I lie in bed
Nearby the car crash is occurring
1991
Young man I'm living with barrels into a tree
Rounds a left curve
4 AM
Foggy
One tree in a field if he winds up skidding off the road
Nothing else to hit
Tree invisible in heavy fog

Barrels with ruler-straight tracks into tree
Death

How would time roll itself up
around
in a No-time setting
An issue no one knows exists
Some sort of quantum gravity in another dimension
Is that what the dream meant?
someplace
where connections match up
possibilities
organize
into PLOTS

January 6, 1991
Old Christmas
34 years old
Death

I dream
Lavender comes in
Deep lavender background
How does it relate? No dots to connect
1991 Death in Belgium
But I find them in time
Jump shot 2005
14 years
Make the connection
Trigger reluctantly pulled
Not wanting to

Was it purposeful?

Pack up
Help write the Hunter Thompson Story
Life purpose
Death purpose
Invisible director
Alpha
Omega
What does it mean?

What was the joy being felt in advance
coming from Hunter in yet another dream shortly before he died
from dreaming of/with Hunter
In No Time
What had occurred?

Agony on Earth
Joy in some dimension
Felt in the dream message
A choice perceived
Timer set

Or rather
A possibility

1991 and earlier, a prior death that fits into the chain
2005—next stop
Or the next of probably many stops

That for some reason is leading up to
A group project of
Writing
The Hunter Thompson Story

It must have other dimensions
Else, why connect it to
Other dimensions?
What are those dimensions up to?

For sure, a lot.
Naturally, I, liking to think like that
Reach up for suspicions like that
Clues,
Mysteries
Bit
To do my part to
Help in the
unfolding

Flash Poem

As if nothing could be done fast enough
In a fever
Mozart
that last year

9

Mystical (Sculpture)

Voyant

O, mighty sculptor
O, poet
as you enter myself like corridors where your paintings hung
and your sculpture stood
as your gigantic hands made to sculpt wouldn't
cannot be
and so you do it even so
you sculpt in pure energy shapes
the shapes of this world
entering now into our world
you sculpt shapes in its presentation
shapes of introduction

you come out of the tombs of the halls of time
with everything
divine

in you
nothing to shape with but the energy
of being
divine

Signature

I stand in a small gallery, staring at the walls of the dining room of
the Tobias School
In the south of England early 1990s

Mesmerized by a signature
It's on a drawing if memory holds
mesmerized by the initials
That feel so familiar
My hands know how to make the exact
Up and down strokes

I can't shake off the notion and years, decades later
Love to re-create it

this signature of initials is known to my hands
It wants to make them—
Up and across in a loop, down deeply in a C
Convoluted
M
Michael
No *A*
Barely an M
supremely conspicuous—the C
Michael
Michaelangelo
Why does no artbook mention this?
At least not that I know of
Has no one been where these prints are held?
My hands practice the signature

The letter C with the flourish at the start
It's an almost unconscious impulse—motion to begin the movement
Michael
Michaelangelo

Unknown signature

How did I know it?
In some collective energy?
Some group energy I reached through focus
Merged with?
As there is nothing but awareness in this focus,
There is no one in it now
A No Mind focus
Into which this awareness of familiarity
Comes
The only person in it in the act of signing his name
Throughout time, as it were,
Michel
angelo

10

In Conclusion

The Verb *To Be*

The verb To Be
ends right here
the end of I *Am*
this is it, The End
for here is Am-O

Defining man now
not I think
I Am-Are

For there is not life without it
no such thing as a definition
of our being
in I Am
Too narrow
The Verb *To Be* has changed—extended into
I Am-Are

Full to capacity
Love in action
AMARE[21]

[21] *amare*—to love (Lat)

Weathering Intensity

The end of *Love in Transition: Voyage of Ulysses—Letters to Penelope* I. Written in Tienen, Belgium, if not in Zurich. If in Tienen, then it was in the energy of what I called "spirit committees," who peopled my solitude in the 1990s.

So that we won't become extinct
like the dinosaurs
when our time comes
to weather enormous intensity of energy
but we will grow from that experience into
A Stronger Species
with runway Lit Up

For I found myself in a dimension that
saw the Earth differently
as stories
constructed from lifetimes
a Homeric structure
a book of the Earth
's untold stories
So that we enter the new century free

Old Close
GONE

In that place
A New
Earth
Close
Found the

Immortal Longings of the Earth
The New
Earth CLOTHES

Silks and satins
Sat-
ins
Having their sit-ins
for The New Earth Close

Andante

In my piano concert, I forgot the end!
Blanked out,
Small figure at the piano at seven
No notes available, limp hands
Excited hands
sat at the piano, started over to play it straight through
beginning to end
patiently, the audience not stirring,
all the time in the world
for Alpha-Omega

        and now for our Earth
    the opening, the Begin, would be,

   "OUI ET"

  "Oui **A/**
ET Non"
There together
banded opposites
 instead of
the clear-cut
forces
of separation.

contrarily minded
Yes—AND
"Oui **A/**
     ET Non"
No

as Answer,
perhaps to the question Baudelaire posed,
that there must be a land where
bread was cake
GOT
TOW

yank, pull, however you want to say it
starting in "and" and this time
a beginning not based on
the forces of
separation

Postscript

I lean and loaf at my ease . . .
observing a spear
of summer grass.

—Whitman

Time

2020,
What are you doing with us?
Surely there could be a more effective way to teach whatever it is
And, by the way, what is it?
What are you teaching—me?

The light cone
its tip pointed out from me
traveling as if blinded
chest open
embracing

to what destination?

at the other point, backwards, tipping into me, my heart

Deliver this! Think!—Hunter S. Thompson

Rethink
Rethink
Rethink
THINK!
This is important!

Think!
Earth
Crew
Ciel

Art of the Christ
The Christ Consciousness Plugged into Taking a Detour into the
Creative Energies

And so the Christ energies (the One with God by any name energies)
Detoured into the Creativity Energies

Ah, my child, what detour is this you speak of?
Detour? We are here all the time
Swarming those who want to hear
These energies roar
Hypersonically down into the Earth
At this time
Landing gear up
On the Way to the Air
Portes

Notes

The Scaffolding on which these poems were built—removed from the text, where they were once intros

Author's Note

While in Morocco (1970–1983) I began to have dreams, then woke and chased down the trails of my night-time images.

> *There is nothing mysterious or metaphysical about the term transcendent function.*
>
> —Carl Jung (1960)

As I was living with my Belgian husband—where French, Spanish, and Arabic were spoken—I experienced, in writing daily, a mélange of languages.

A major dream in the early 1980s: *I was writing and reached routinely for a blank page but couldn't find one. At that instant the light came on, showing me I had been writing in the dark before; marveling, I saw that the only pages left to write on held never-before-seen (i.e., unconscious) paintings on a wall. Portraits of whom?* No matter. *The paintings filled the remaining pages I'd assumed were blank. I gaped. Why had no one ever seen this illustrious art? I watched as first, on an earlier half-page, then another half-page and another, my writing vanished. An invisible hand replaced it with scenes.*

Finally, I saw myself on a stage, receiving the award for my book—I have no idea the size of the audience: large or miniscule—"of Number

Four this century because it was rare." What a perplexing, astonishing grade from the unconscious. Where had the pictures been? In the unconscious but for how long? They had looked to me like Old Masters. For Jung, *number four—was?* "An instinct of individuation," he said, i.e., "of wholeness."

From then on, I was on the lookout for these unknown portraits and scenes I had seen replace text with pictures, as if pulled down by an unseen hand. Also, on the lookout to suddenly "wake up."

I think the archetype of four depends on—in my case—clever that the unconscious is—making "rare" identical with H<u>arre</u>ll.

Posterity was no longer "on call." I had to excavate my garage boxes. Dig up this deluge of poetry. Waiting. Thus not go AWOL from history, my fault.

From the Nothingness of Thin Air

Written in 2001

Milton Klonsky is a key influence in my life and thus in the *Keep This Quiet!* series. Below is an introduction of sorts. Considered a guru/ hipster (or, as he preferred, a "gangster poet"), and "with an IQ that can stutter your butter," as author Seymour Krim, his close friend and acolyte put it, he always spoke in quotable phrases, such as

> *I'm famous, not so much for what I've written . . . as for the cyclotron of my personality.*
>
> *I'm a teabag, steeped in life.*
>
> *I'm like an airplant, not rooted in anything. Certainly not in earth.*

Measurement Poems

Written while testing the energy in my apartment with a random number generator given me by a Netherlands physicist, Dick Bierman, for that purpose. In the same period, I went to Ibiza for a light body seminar, where the experience described in this poem happened.

A Dash of French

> It was not only Hemingway that Margaret Harrell went to see at the Dôme Restaurant; it was Charlie Baudelaire—discovering the unconscious link with his poem *Le Gâteau*.
>
> —Eugène van Itterbeek, professor of French literature/poet/ publisher la Maison Européene de la Poésie

The FIRE Side of the Home Plot

Written in 1991 during a sublet near La Honda, California, after a kundalini incident opened up blocks.

I suddenly felt the unmistakable shaking of kundalini kriyas—— while reading Kahlil Gibran's Miriam (Mary Magdalene) story ("On Meeting Jesus for the First Time") in his *Jesus the Son of Man: By Those Who Knew Him*. They began at the exact passage, "And I remember Him pacing the evening. He was not walking. He Himself was a road above the road; even as a cloud above the earth that would descend to refresh the earth. But when I stood before

Him and spoke to him, He was a man, and His face was powerful to behold. And He said to me, 'What would you, Miriam?'

Instantly, I found myself before a council (preceding my birth), deciding my life purpose.

Meanwhile, the face of guru Dhyanyogi-ji peered out at me from the wall calendar of the apartment I was renting from Jyoti, who was with him in India.

At the same time I was basking in the afterglow of a visit to Owl Farm, where I saw Hunter Thompson in person for the first time in twenty-one years. I had him on my mind, writing notes (most unmailed) in between some of these poems; telling him I had a "Go signal" and it was for him too. He, meanwhile, was roaring away on *Fear and Loathing in Elko*.

The insertion "D I D" was a tiny example of the "computer PK" in my Tienen, Belgium, apartment just beginning, fledglingly, in 1991 but which ran through the 1990s. My apartment was humming— filled-to-the-rafters—with spirit activity, peculiarly training me through the "computer PK" that modified the on-screen text in the printouts. Technically, PK is *mind influencing matter*, as in spoon bending. The same page might reprint totally differently the next time, creating another focus, another emphasis, or a graphic design made from the words. I was mightily impressed.

Atelier Dante

> Like a female Joyce, Harrell is attracted by the etymologies that can substitute for the logos; therefore, fascinated by the concavities of notions, which can substitute for the non-spatiality of the logos.
>
> —Ion Mircea, 2012 winner of the Mihai Eminescu Poetry Life Achievement Award, "Opera Omnia"

A cosmic spirit poured these poems into my consciousness in *The Christ State*, written with me way above my then-consciousness. As spelled out into my awareness back then, the Earth was barreling toward the twenty-first century, with most of the inhabitants unaware of the challenges it raced toward. Robert, protagonist of *Love in Transition*, is the fictionalized Milton. Newly departed, perceived as a super-conscious spirit relaying messages back down to me on Earth, he uses his death to catapult me into a serious investigation of consciousness, bringing me messages for the Earth. Messages, stories, from The Christ State pertinent—urgent—now.

To the Earth

These are poems from *The Christ State*

Jung Institute Initiation 1985–1986

At the C. G. Jung Institute Zurich, I had an initiation—or "Confrontation with the Self"—brought to me in the Christ consciousness by a spirit guide, writing together with me a book of poetry, published in Romania in 1996: *Love in Transition* III: *The Christ State*. Robert is the male protagonist in *Love in Transition* I–

II—semi-modeled on New York City "gangster poet"/guru Milton Klonsky; from the first day I met him, he was part-mentor (his was the most phenomenal mind I'd ever met), part-romantic interest (reluctantly on my part). It was at Milton's death in 1981 that everything in my life accelerated 1000 percent, as it appeared to me—astonishingly—that he was hanging around to guide me in spirit in a much-expanded form. Was that possible? On the other hand, could such a mind wither away, crumble into dust? And if it didn't, what would it say? Well, first of all, it was much expanded, though not so much more than I am right now, these many decades later. For I imbibed and then digested these revelations and teachings.

I took him to be the much larger form of Klonsky, whose death in November 1981—from the instant I intuited it had happened till I confirmed the fact in mid-1982—created an agonizing void in me, as he had occupied a pole of my reality I called "the Highest Truth." Now that pole was vacant unless I filled it myself.

But as if to give me more pointers before leaving me to that task, in an elaborate first appearance in my studio apartment in Zurich, he convinced me he had not left—just changed form—offering me a personalized entry into a vibration he called "the Christ State," or the Christ Spirit or consciousness. A level of consciousness within and available to every human being, by any name. I had yet to learn much about Hinduism, Buddhism, etc.

However, it was concerned to be received on its own terms, authentically, not diluted or translated. Then cause-effect would be askew because the cause of an attraction or event would be assumed to be local, when in fact, it might be—often was—coming from Another Dimension. Stepping down a vibration to bring it into this dimension was a process that regularly occurred—positively. But could backfire—if unconscious.

144

This danger was impressed upon me as of importance as the Earth went to a higher vibration. In that approaching period, vibrations that had been personified might cause real havoc if released—to assist the Earth—but caught up in ego and unconscious misusage. Naturally, I took all this to heart and sometimes probably exaggerated, in my mind, the dangers to those masters themselves, which I felt great reverence for.

The "two Christs" is a reference to the outer personality; i.e., the serious Jesus personality we are all familiar with was joined by a new, more playful outer expression, fronting for the same inner core. In the initiation I was introduced to this second outer personality type, exemplified in the sometimes-fun-loving Mozart.

A second major theme of *The Christ State* was to create a pattern or models for the Sacred Marriage.

In sum: the outwardly chaotic scene was mirroring something starkly different.

A Good Show

This poetry compounds the word play, illustrating cosmic humor and linguistic unity, underneath which it is serious indeed.

Mystical Writings
From *Love in Transition*, Vol II

Written in Zurich, and Belgium, 1985–1995 published 1996 in Romania

Poems about/after the death of Milton Klonsky—after the changes I underwent in the initiation in Zurich that introduced me to his larger self, to mine as well, mystical writings about encounters and connection, as he had told me—in his larger self—to look for him not in outer form but inner being expression. What an assignment. How?

Remembering Hunter S. Thompson (mostly)

I was Hunter's copyeditor/assistant editor for his first book, *Hell's Angels*, which rocketed him into the national spotlight. We became fast friends, and I saved his letters to me—published forty years later in the first two volumes of *Keep This Quiet!* Despite the popularity of the wildman Hunter Figure, there is a less-publicized way to look at him, detected brilliantly by internationally acclaimed poet Ron Whitehead: as a shaman.

Mystical (Sculpture)
Voyant

Upon sensing a long-"dead" artist/mystic in a meditation in the 1990s—Michelangelo, to be exact, as in that deep trance I was in, the unconscious attraction was to "the Great Artist," representing the entry of whatever energy it was I felt in the convulsive depths; a name I gave it, in the gravity that brought it there, helping me find that depth—the beyond-3D.

Acknowledgments

I am thankful for all the breaks I received, which did not always seem so at the time. First, thankful for the warm, inspiring parents and family I was born into; thankful for meeting Virginia Parrott Williams at Duke, who stood by me in helping me get my books out all these years; whose insightful eye told me "in" and "out" often when I asked her for an opinion on paragraphs. And that was just the beginning. For the C. G. Jung Institute (and Jung himself), whose foundation served me well and where I was introduced to lifelong friends, champions of the Earth and its indigenous teachings, Jyoti and Russell Park, as well as Pui Harvey (all with PhD beside their names and warmth in their hearts); thankful for my friends in Belgium and in New York City and those at Kayumari. For Didi-Ionel Cenuser, who acted as my publisher for years and years in Romania, friend, author in his own right; for the friends I met after moving back to Raleigh, NC. The marvelous new openings they showed me. For friends in the Gonzo world, who unexpectedly opened wide their hearts, minds, art, and friendship to me. Two of these being Ron Whitehead and Tim Denevi, who both encouraged me to bring out this book, Tim in the very early stages, Ron later, suggesting ways to take out the clutter of too much explanation. Naturally, to poet Alice Osborn, who first told me, *Margaret, you should collect your poems*, and then curated which ones to include here. And family, most notably my two sisters and cousin Noel Baucom. And that's just the start. Thanks for the privilege of this lifetime.

Coming Soon

If you find these images intriguing—if the sky calls you—be on the lookout for my next book (short, deep, and fanciful) filled with sky images, called *Cloud Conversations & Image Stories— Leonardo's Theory*.

Sign up on https://margaretharrell.com/news/ for Announcements and other news updates for my readers.

Key Events

1965, Montparnasse, Paris: Sat down at the Dôme Café with the intent to begin writing the Big Book. Saw a clown-beggar, asking in mime for a cigarette. He pulled a trigger, as it were, and I started *Love in Transition* (untitled).

1965, 1966: Met Milton Klonsky, then Hunter S. Thompson in New York City. Physically met Hunter in March 1967.

1965–'68: Worked at Random House, from hence the story below took off.

1980: Began recording dreams and working daily on the images in Morocco.

1981: Witnessed a Belgian parade at roughly the same time Milton Klonsky died in New York City.

1985: Had a seminal Zurich Initiation. Wrote *The Christ State*.

1990s: Finished *Love in Transition* in Tienen, Belgium—accompanied by the Computer "PK." The boyfriend who shared the apartment died in January 1991.

1991: Went to Owl Farm to see Hunter S. Thompson in person in May the first time in twenty-one years.

1991: Had a kundalini flashback in California at a sublet of Jyoti (Jeneane Prevatt) while she was in India three months.

1993: Read a long poem, "Invocation to Masters of the Past," in an international poetry festival in Romania, making friends with a few poets, such as Mark Strand.

1996: Saw publication of *Love in Transition* I–II and *The Christ State* in Romania.

2001: Went to Ibiza and "journeyed" in meditation with the light body teacher, Roland Verschave, at which time Milton Klonsky stepped out front from inside my "soul grouping" and gave the message, Measure me.

2001: Relocated to the U.S.

2005: Was the year Hunter S. Thompson died.

2005: Was the year *Toward a Philosophy of Perception: The Magnitude of Human Potential* was published.

2011–2018: Saw publication of *Keep This Quiet!* I–IV in the U.S. by Saeculum University Press, parent office in Romania.

2020 and 2021: Saw publication of *The* Hell's Angels *Letters: Hunter S. Thompson, Margaret Harrell and the Making of an American Classic*, in collaboration with Ron Whitehead.

Selected Reviews

"We can't have a John Done living today."

—Professor William Blackburn, 1962

Upon reading pages of my history Honors and Distinction paper as a twenty-year-old Duke University student

No, no, he said. John Donne today?
We cannot have it.

Who? I thought.
Bursting into tears.
John Donne?
Who was that?
Not me. Not me.

Poetry

"From when I first again saw her in 1983 until the present 1995, I have watched Margaret devote her life to her project, the first part of which is printed here. Poetry and metaphysical vision, *Love in Transition* is the cry through Margaret's soul to the twenty-first century. Highly recommended for its vision, fierce intelligence and great literary merit."
—Virginia Parrott Williams, PhD, author of *Surrealism, Quantum Philosophy, and World War I*; coauthor of the best-selling *Anger Kills*

Love in Transition: Voyage of Ulysses— Letters to Penelope I

"Her book does have the quality of "logical, integrated thought"; it is always in control of its widely diverse factual and imaginative material. . . . I only wish I could read it with a small class as I repeatedly did with James Joyce's *Ulysses*. Her book deserves such close study."

—Harold Parker, PhD, Professor Emeritus of History,
Duke University

**

The *Keep This Quiet!* Series

Keep This Quiet! I

"Addictive" and "a delight."
—Mark Strand, former U.S. Poet Laureate

"Margaret Harrell's *Keep This Quiet!* offers an illuminating look at Hunter S. Thompson in full throttle trying to make it as a Top Notch prose-stylist. Harrell fills in many important biographical gaps. A welcome addition to what is becoming the HST cottage industry. Read it."

—Douglas Brinkley, editor of *The Proud Highway* and *Fear and Loathing in America*

"Memoir will likely please Hunter S. Thompson fans and appeal to readers with an interest in the beginnings of the post-modern era or the personal sacrifices involved in bringing serious written work to fruition."

—*Kirkus Indie Reviews*

"With a solid dose of humor and another perspective on these writers from a personal friend, *Keep This Quiet!* is a moving read and much recommended to any literary studies or memoir collection."

—*Midwest Book Review*

"KEEP THIS QUIET! a memoir: *My Relationship with Hunter S. Thompson, Milton Klonsky, and Jan Mensaert* by Margaret A. Harrell is a masterpiece! I never expected to say that about a memoir."

—Ron Whitehead, outlaw poet

"In the ever-expanding list of biographies and memoirs about Hunter S. Thompson, this latest offering, *Keep This Quiet!* by Margaret A. Harrell, is quite simply a breath of fresh air. . . . What sets *Keep This Quiet!* apart is the extent to which Harrell explores the question of identity and myth, in her quest to simultaneously answer questions concerning her own character and that of one Hunter S. Thompson. As Harrell writes early on—"Who was he? There was no indication how complicated that answer was."

—Rory Feehan, PhD, owner of https://totallygonzo.org

"Three men, embodiments of three different dimensions of the late 1960's Zeitgeist—wispy dissolution, language-charged intellect, and Gonzo persona-building—are brought together by Harrell to invoke a world of passion and commitment . . . *Keep This Quiet!* is at once noisy, sensual, and word-drunk, as well as quietly intimate and full of Harrell's wonder at her luck. While most readers will come to this book for the Thompson content, in truth all the portraits here—all four of them—are compelling and often touching."

— W. C. Bamberger, *Rain Taxi Review*

"This is no ordinary book about or including Thompson. It's a memoir detailing personal relationships with three authors, the main focus being on Hunter. . . . [I] must stress that this book, as a memoir is quite deep and holds the door open for the reader. While Hunter is a huge selling point, the book has the legs to stand alone."

—Martin Flynn, owner of https://hstbooks.org

Representative Reviews—*Keep <u>THIS</u> Quiet Too!*—IV, rev. ed.

Keep <u>THIS</u> Quiet Too!

"A passionately written memoir that doesn't sit around being fit and proper and straight-laced. If I can use a well-worn phrase here, 'it lifts the lid on so many things.' . . . As a key to the lives of these three writers it is idiosyncratic and in age where blandness is the norm it is a pleasure to go on her journey and find out a little about what made these men tick and what drove her to them."

—*Beat Scene* (UK print magazine)

Keep This Quiet! III

"This is the third and highly recommended title in Margaret Harrell's outstanding *Keep This Quiet!* autobiographical series. A fascinating and very well written personal story, *Keep This Quiet!* III: *Initiations* is very highly recommended for both community and academic library collections. Also exceptionally commended are the first two volumes in this outstanding series, *Keep This Quiet! My Relationship with Hunter S. Thompson, Milton Klonsky, and Jan Mensaert,* and *Keep THIS Quiet Too!*"

—*Midwest Book Review*

"As though it arrived with a full legion of angelic messengers and masters of light, from the moment I touched this book, its energy began to flow through me. If you are ready to welcome energetic shifts toward enlightenment, this book is for you. This beautifully written volume of wisdom provides attunements as you meander through its pages joining Margaret on her journey."

—Diana Henderson, author of *Grandfather Poplar*

"Margaret Harrell's blending and merging the whole of a human being and beyond into the cosmos is astounding writing and what a lifetime Journey she has taken to arrive to this book. I feel Margaret is zipping around and catching the flavors of the world, the universe and Beyond. She is working with a whole new and different combined East-West and Middle Paradigm."

—Suzanne V. Brown, PhD, psychologist, former VP, Exceptional Human Experience

"Margaret Harrell is a skilled professional writer with excellent ability to communicate and weave esoteric ideas about science, psychology, philosophy, and spirituality. Richard Unger's channeled hand analysis description of her as a 'grand synthesizer' was apt and accurate."

—Ron Rattner, author of the forthcoming *From Litigation to Meditation: An ex-lawyer's spiritual metamorphosis from secular Hebrew to born again Hindu to uncertain Undo*

The Hell's Angels *Letters: Hunter S. Thompson, Margaret Harrell and the* Making of an American Classic

"Thompson's motto might well have been 'Nothing in moderation.' For *The Hell's Angels Letters*, Margaret Ann Harrell—in collaboration with Ron Whitehead—has assembled a dossier of all her correspondence with Thompson during the time she worked as the editor of the gonzo writer's 'strange and terrible saga of the outlaw motorcycle gangs.' Typed manuscript pages, scribbled notes, photographs, interviews and all sorts of period ephemera relating to *Hell's Angels* allow the reader a valuable, behind-the-scenes glimpse into the making of this classic of New Journalism."

—Michael Dirda, the *Washington Post*

"As the title implies, this book is mainly comprised of letters between Harrell and Thompson, some typed and some handwritten, and all printed here in colour. Of course, there are already two collections of Hunter Thompson's letters available, but somehow they are even more enjoyable when read in the original form. Whether typed or scrawled in giant letters with a red pen, Thompson's correspondence is invariably annotated and corrected in his unique way, adding a layer of personality that was missing from the collections, as well—of course—as Harrell's explanations that provide further insight."

—David Wills, *Beatdom*

"This is a big book, literally and figuratively. The short version:

"*The Hell's Angels Letters* is a must-have text for any Hunter S. Thompson fan. Lavishly documented and illustrated with the actual correspondence that led to the publication of his breakthrough literary effort, *Hell's Angels*, this coffee-table book literally shows how HST boot-strapped his way from a impoverished nobody journalist to growing legend. The author, Margaret Harrell, who was Thompson's editor on his inaugural book, and her collaborator, Thompson's friend and associate poet Ron Whitehead, have succeeded brilliantly to create a fabulous present for you, or anyone in your life who admires Thompson's numerous achievements. It is not inexpensive, but no matter, it's worth every penny. *The* Hell's Angels *Letters: Hunter S Thompson, Margaret Harrell and the Making of an American Classic* gets five stars out of five! Bravo!"

—Kyle K. Mann, *Gonzo Today*

Also by Margaret A. Harrell

The Hell's Angels *Letters: Hunter S. Thompson, Margaret Harrell and the Making of an American Classic*—in collaboration with Ron Whitehead

Keep This Quiet!
Keep THIS Quiet Too!
Keep This Quiet! III
Keep This Quiet! IV, rev. ed.

Toward a Philosophy of Perception

Marking Time with Faulkner—Literary Criticism

Space Encounters volumes I–III

Love in Transition volumes I–IV

About the Author

Margaret Ann Harrell was born in North Carolina and educated academically at Duke University (BA) and Columbia University (MA). She did postgraduate work at the C. G. Jung Institute in Zurich (1984–'87), followed by energy studies and investigations that continue to this day. Since, in late 2001, after thirty adventurous years abroad in Morocco and Europe, she moved back to the United States, she has been an advanced-meditation light-body teacher—most recently a luminous-body teacher—in the Orin & DaBen LuminEssence work.

Margaret was a copyeditor/assistant editor at Random House, New York City, often to first-book writers who later became prominent, such as Hunter S. Thompson. Introduced to parapsychology by Dr. J. B. Rhine at Duke University, she eventually found a part of her calling in exploring the meaning and boundaries of consciousness/unconsciousness. She is a three-time fellow at MacDowell Colony.

Margaret is in demand as a speaker. Most recently, at the launch at the Canessa Gallery in San Francisco in July 2021 of her latest book, *The* Hell's Angels *Letters: Hunter S. Thompson, Margaret Harrell and the Making of an American Classic*, in collaboration with Ron Whitehead, US National Beat Poet Laureate. Earlier, she authored the four-volume memoir series *Keep This Quiet!* (Saeculum University Press 2011–'18). And before that, published in Sibiu, Romania, in English, the seven-volume nonfiction *Love in Transition* and the *Space Encounters* series.

In cloud photography, exhibited now and then in Romania, Italy, Bruges (Belgium), and New York City, she is fascinated with the sun. Her biography and photographs were also many times in

Marquis *Who's Who in Modern American Art*. For several years she has been a VIP presenter at the Gonzofest (Louisville). Margaret, a longtime freelance book editor, now edits additionally for authors in the Self-Publishing School. For a fuller picture of her, see https://margaretharrell.com.

Thank You for Reading My Book

Authors live by readers and their reviews. If you enjoyed *Particle Piñata Poems*, I would deeply appreciate an honest positive review on Amazon and/or other platform. I will read every word you write and benefit from the comments. Thank you again and God bless.

www.ingramcontent.com/pod-product-compliance
Lightning Source LLC
Chambersburg PA
CBHW040854120626
46551CB00001B/16